Blue

A play

Heather Dunmore

Samuel French — London

www.samuelfrench-london.co.uk

FOR AMATEUR PRODUCTION ENQUIRIES

UNITED KINGDOM AND WORLD EXCLUDING NORTH AMERICA

plays@samuelfrench.co.uk

020 7255 4302/01

Each title is subject to availability from Samuel French, depending upon country of performance.

CHARACTERS

Leo, a professional man in his mid-forties – also
plays himself aged 7, 11 and 32
Leo's Mother, aged 46, 50, 70 and 79
Rachel, Leo's wife, aged 40
Frances, Leo's sister, aged 39
Patient
Hypnotherapist
Hospital Nurse
Art Therapist

Rachel, the **Hospital Nurse** and the **Hypnotherapist** can
all be played by one person.

Frances, the **Patient** and the **Art Therapist** can all be
played by one person.

SCENE 1

Lights up on Leo, sitting in an armchair wearing glasses. He looks unkempt and worried

There is another chair and a table with a telephone on it. To one side or the rear of the stage there is a bed

Leo stares at the wall for several seconds in silence. Then he turns to face the audience

Leo (*reflecting*) I ignored it for a while—tried to shrug it off. (*Pause*) I kept it from Rachel. I didn't want to worry her; she had enough to think about—I lost weight too. Still—I needed to. Everything started to taste the same—just couldn't raise the enthusiasm. It was the same with golf—gradually it was as if everything had lost its colour—even sex. (*Pause*) Rachel couldn't understand it—I wouldn't have minded but she was never that keen before. She made me go and see old Saunders. Lot of good he was. Talked about the "blues", I said to him "Saunders, old chap, there's nothing blue about my world, my world is completely grey." He told me to take a holiday.

Silence

I felt tired all the time. I kept waking up earlier and earlier and just as it was time to get up I'd start to drop off. What had begun as worry turned into fear and the fear into anxiety—I know all about that. It's only fear when you know what you're frightened of. With anxiety it's a whole new ball game. It's anything and everything and most of it trivial and insignificant and not worth worrying about. When you're feeling OK, that is——

The telephone rings, interrupting him

Rachel enters

Rachel Are you going to answer it?

Leo doesn't answer

(*Picking up the phone*) Hello ... Oh, hello Frances. ... (*Looking at Leo*) Yes, very busy ... you know Leo. ... How is the poor old thing?... Oh dear, well, I'll tell him... Bye, Frances. (*Putting the receiver down*) You really should go and see your mother, Leo.
Leo Mmm.

Silence

Rachel I thought we might have Jack and Izzy round—it's ages since we've seen them. (*Pause*) Leo? (*Pause*) You wouldn't have to do anything—or we could go out—Sara would keep an eye on Mattie. (*After a long pause, speaking louder*) Leo? We'll have no friends left soon. (*Silence*) Are you going to sit there all day again?
Leo I don't know.

Rachel exits

Sound of an outside door banging

(*Calling out in a feeble, weak voice*) Don't be long.

Leo looks around him as if he suspects that there is someone watching him. Finally he sits down on the floor and hugs himself, rocking backwards and forwards

A spotlight goes up on another part of the stage where Mother (aged 79) is in a hospital bed

She sits up very slowly, folding back the sheet on the bed and swings her legs over the side of the bed to face the audience. Leo cannot see her but she appears to be able to see him

Mother (*age 79*) I never really believed that hearing is the last sense to go but it's true, you know. I just lie here day after day and all I can do is listen—yes, listen. Apart from that, my body simply refuses to function. (*Pause*) It's like my legs and arms aren't part of me— yet every sound—I sometimes wonder is this the final retribution? The nurses understand—but the rest—Joyce and Eileen popped in yesterday— (*Mimicking*) "She can't hear you dear—I said she can't hear you dear,"—I can't tell you how frustrating that is especially when that's the signal to start tearing you apart in whispers. But I can hear, you see. Whispers are especially easy to pick up by the trained ear. And these ears are in serious training. I mean serious training. What else is there to do? (*Pause*) At least they moved me out of the ward—all those dotty old dears—"I'm eighty four, you know—" More like a hundred and four I'd have said. They've probably spent most of their lives lying about their age, now they can't stop bragging about it. (*Pause*) It's so dark in here. Claustrophobia's been the bane of my life. Frances comes to see me and reads me her dreadful novellas—(*Sadly*) but the boys never come. (*Beat*) They've fitted me with a catheter now. (*Lifting her nightdress to reveal a catheter attached to her leg*) And that was all I was after— (*Pause*) Every couple of hours a nice male nurse turns me over—to stop the bedsores, you saucy things—to stop the bedsores and to feed me disgusting pink liquid straight into my stomach. He just pours it out of a plastic jug into a funnel—At least it cuts out the middleman—I wish they'd stop. But what can I do? I can't speak now—nothing comes out. Waiting—waiting for death. I wish he'd hurry up. (*She sits back on the bed*)

The spotlight on her dims

Leo reflects and turns to face the audience

Leo I don't know whose idea it was—some misguided soul—a form of shock treatment perhaps...

Tape (*child's voice*) "Are we nearly there, Daddy?"

Leo No.

Tape (*child's voice*) "Are we nearly there?"

Leo You just asked that question.

Tape (*child's voice*) "Yes, but are we?"

Leo We've just passed High Wycombe.

Tape (*child's voice*) "Where's Hi Wycle, Daddy?"

Leo Wycombe, it's HIGH WYCOMBE.

Tape (*child's voice, slowly*) "Hi Wick Um—but we're nearly there?"

Leo Yes. Let me concentrate now. There's a lot of traffic.

Tape (*child's voice*) "How long till we get there?"

Leo Another two hours.

Tape (*child's voice*) "But you said we were nearly there——"

Leo I know.

Tape (*child's voice*) "Is this the right way, Daddy? (*Pause*) Are you sure this is the right way? (*Pause*) What's the matter? Why have you stopped? (*Pause*) You can't stop here, Daddy. (*Pause*) Those people are making faces at us—(*Pause*) You're frightening me, Daddy— (*Starting to cry*) I want to go home—"

Leo (*reflecting*) I've had a few more panic attacks since then, but luckily no more in the fast lane of the M40. (*Pause*) Somehow I got the car onto the hard shoulder—sweat pouring off me—pulse racing—heart thumping in my chest like a drum—(*Pause*) I told Mattie it was a game—I don't think he believed me. Kids are brighter than that—and now he doesn't trust me either. We never got to Thorpe Park—there didn't seem any point—I'd been dreading it anyway.

Silence

Mother had been depressed for years—all her life probably, though she'd never have admitted it. Physically, she'd always been as strong as an ox—she'd go on forever...

Lights up on Mother (aged 46)

Leo either hides behind a chair and plays the scene as an anxious seven-year-old or alternatively he stands a few feet away from Mother while she talks to a space in front of both her and him – as if they are both remembering him as a young boy. They continue to stare at the space – which with them makes up a triangle – throughout all of the speeches in this section

Mother (*aged 46*) Leo, there you are! Where have you been? I told you we were leaving at two.

Leo (*aged 7*) I—I—I—d—don't want to go...

Mother (*aged 46*) I hope you're not going to be silly. There are plenty of little boys would give their eye-teeth to be in your position...

Leo (*aged 7*) You—you don't know what it's like.

Mother (*aged 46*) Come on now! (*Pause*) You do look a bit pale—have you got your rubber sheet?

Leo (aged 7) They'll put me in the baby dorm again.

Mother (*aged 46*; *After a pause*) I hope you're not going to be sick in the car.

Leo (*aged 7*; *desperately*) I—I don't feel very well...

Sound of a car horn

Mother (*aged 46*) Oh dear, that's your father. You know what happens if we keep him waiting...

Lights down on Mother

Leo (*reflecting*) I knew I ought to visit Mother in the hospital but I only ever went out to pick up a prescription from Saunders. I told him "I know what's in them—you can't fob me off like your average punter." "Probably a darn sight better than the stuff you're prescribing for yourself" he said. He's no fool—'though he kept offering me Viagra. (*Shaking his head*) Viagra! God knows what he doles out for the common cold. Poor old Saunders—(*Pause*) Had I been like that?

Leo starts to look confident and in control

A female patient enters and sits down in the other chair opposite him

Leo Could be any number of things. Probably viral. Life getting on top of you.

Patient I feel tired all the time, Doctor.

Leo I expect you're overdoing it.

Patient All I do is sleep...

Leo How about finding yourself an interest. What do you like doing?

Patient That's just it—nothing interests me anymore.

Leo A bit of retail therapy usually does it for my wife.

Patient I'm on benefit...

Leo Oh. (*Pause*) An evening class? Flower arranging or something – or you could get your husband to take you out somewhere nice?

Patient My husband left me...

Leo Well, of course that's it, isn't it! I am sorry—but these things take time. When—did he ...?

Patient It's been a little over fifteen years.

Leo Fifteen years! (*Collecting himself*) Fifteen years—you allergic to anything? This'll help you sleep. (*Writing a prescription*) New on the market. Take two before you go to bed. They're quite safe. (*Holding out the prescription*) Give this to the pharmacist on your way out.

The patient starts to leave

Fifteen years!

The patient exits

Leo looks timid and lost again. He stares at the wall for a few seconds

Crossfade to followspot on Mother (aged 79) who gets up and moves around jauntily, talking to the audience

Mother (*aged 79*) You'd think they'd at least come and see me—Leo's only just down the motorway. I'm glad I'm not his patient. I'd be long gone waiting for him to show up. Long gone. (*Pause*) You spend half your life raising them and what for? Imminent death is very sobering. When I think what else I might have done with my life?

She starts to dance

I wanted to be a dancer—entertaining the troops—(*Kicking her legs up in the air*) high-kicking my way around the world—taking the bows as the flowers hit the stage—(*Wryly*) I suppose that's out now. The Colonel, even Mother called him that, thought there was something rather infra dig about the stage so he made sure he married me off to someone "eminently suitable" pretty damn quick. But marriage and Motherhood are no substitute—I was never very good at either—No substitute. Not when you want to perform—when you want to be up there—under the lights—(*Pause*) I was a star at the local am-dram—well, I helped with the costumes... The leading man and the producer were having a bit of a thing. Opened my eyes... (*Looking up and sighing*) Oh—here comes Frances—oh no, she's carrying one of her library books again—"Entering the room in his naval uniform, Maurice looked every inch the gentleman. *Every* inch! Yet there was an unmistakable caddish quality to him. When their eyes met across the gallery, Lorena knew she was lost..." I don't think I can stand it.

Crossfade followspot down on Mother and lights back up on Leo

Leo reflects and turns to face the audience

Leo I'd always favoured the Socks School of Psychology myself. So it irritated me that I couldn't seem to pull up my own. And I couldn't put my finger on why. They might be closing down the Health Centre. Just a "might" at this stage—no real cause for alarm—I'd get something else—but in my mind I'd built it up out of all proportion and my self-confidence was ebbing away. (*Pause*) Round about the same time, Peter Barraclough pipped me to the post—nine years I'd been President—and instead of continuing to fall, my handicap was out of control. Rachel kept nagging me about starting the patio—picking the kids up from their endless activities—lunch with Mother—putting the lid back on the sauce bottle—it was all too much trouble. (*Silence*) When Doug retired they went over my head and took on a new partner—young chap—too clever by half—don't ask me why but I got it into my head that people I'd happily worked alongside for years were plotting against me—luring my patients away—challenging my diagnoses—falsifying blood tests. The writing was on the wall... (*Pause*) Still, chin up. Soldier on. Tomorrow's another day. Trouble was tomorrow was exactly like yesterday. Everything was slowing down to a full stop. Getting out of bed was like scaling Everest. The thought of going to see Mother in the hospital was unendurable. The endless procession of sick human beings through the surgery just about put the tin hat on it—So I stopped going in...

The doorbell rings

Leo gets up slowly to answer the door

Frances enters and sits

Leo Frances! Well, this is a surprise!
Frances (*after a pause*) I really only popped in on my way to pick up Josh from Uni. (*Pause*) It's just that you haven't been to see Mother—and I can never get you on the phone.
Leo I've been meaning to...
Frances I know she misses you. (*Pause*) You always were her favourite...
Leo I don't know where you got that idea.

Silence

Frances Have you lost weight?
Leo Just a few pounds. (*Beat*) Good thing too. Has Simon been in—to see Mother?
Frances He's in Dubai until June. He has sent some beautiful flowers. I'm sure he'll go in as soon as he gets back.
Leo Ever the dutiful son…
Frances So you see it's been down to me. I do the best I can—It's not even as if she knows what's going on—just lies there—oblivious—in her own little world, shut off from everything—

Leo She might quite like that.

Frances What a peculiar thing to say...

Leo As I remember, she was always disappearing for "a little lie down".

Frances That's not fair. Poor mummy—it was her nerves.

Leo At least it'll keep her off the booze.

Frances I'll ignore that.

Leo Why not? Everyone else does.

Frances I ought to be going.

Leo Sure you don't want a coffee? (*More enthusiastically*) Drink? I should have offered before...

Frances (*raising her eyebrows and getting up to go*) At ten in the morning?

Frances exits

Leo heaves a long sigh of relief. He's clearly worn out by the whole process of deception and slumps back in the chair exhausted

Leo (*reflecting*) Rachel was really worried. Inertia had taken over. My lethargy almost amounted to paralysis. She'd been in to see Mother—but I just couldn't raise the energy—'though I kept thinking about her—Rachel thought I'd never work again—thought she'd be pushing me around in a bath chair for the next thirty years. All she could say was "At least you're not violent". I began to wonder if she wished I were. It might have broken the monotony. It might at least have given her a reason to leave me—

Leo pulls a hip flask, concealed down the back of the chair, and swigs from it, then stuffs it back quickly

Rachel enters with Leo's unopened mail

Rachel You haven't opened your mail. (*Pause*) D'you want me to sort it out?

Leo I don't care.

Rachel Well, I care. I care if the electricity gets cut off and the house is repossessed—

Leo It won't come to that.

Rachel How would you know? All you do is sit in that chair staring at the wall.

Leo Frances has tired me out.

Rachel I wouldn't mind but if I want to go out you can't handle it. (*Beat*) The kids don't understand—they miss you—even though you're never out of our sight. The house is like a morgue. Josie will dream up any excuse to go out. Sara hides in her room—if it weren't for Mattie—

Leo I know I'm useless. I don't know why you don't just kick me out.

Rachel Don't start that again. I'm not in the mood—

Leo I mean it. I'm pathetic.

Rachel (*shouting*) Just shut up, will you? For nineteen years you've divided your time between work, the Rotary Club and the golf course. All of a sudden I'm expected to deal with you twenty-four hours a day. Well, it's not easy.

Leo Are you saying you're leaving?

Rachel Don't be ridiculous.

Leo No, seriously—

Rachel All I'm saying is the sight of you in that chair is driving me mad—I can't go out and I can't stay in. The bills are mounting up and all you can do is sit there and feel sorry for yourself.

Leo I can't help it.

Rachel If they close the Health Centre now, you'll be first out the door and then where will we be?

Leo They can't do that.

Rachel Look, I'm sorry. I'm trying to understand. I'm doing my best. I'm trying to hold everything together here. Trying to carry on as normal but every now and then I blow—It's partly the pretence— You won't talk to me and I can't talk to anyone else about it either. It's driving me mad!

Leo starts crying

Oh my God! Don't do that! (*Shouting*) You're a bloody doctor for Christ's sake, sort yourself out!

Rachel exits, slamming the door

Leo (*reflecting*) There's one split second in every day—that moment when you wake up—before it all comes flooding back and drags you down. After that it's like drowning very slowly...

Lights up on Mother (aged 50) with a school report in her hand

Either Leo plays this scene as an eleven-year-old, starting with him getting up and kicking a football around or alternatively both he and Mother stand a few feet away from each other both staring at a space— which with them makes up a triangle—in front of them. They continue to stare at the space throughout all of the speeches in this section

Mother (*aged 50*) Your father wants to see you!
Leo (*aged 11*) (*spotting the report*) Oh.
Mother (*aged 50*) At this rate you'll never get into Med. School, Leo—and it's not as if you haven't got the ability...
Leo (*aged 11*) I'm only eleven.
Mother (*aged 50; reading*) "Leo is a quiet, well-mannered boy who would benefit from more active participation in class discussions."
Leo (*aged 11*) What's that?
Mother (*aged 50*) Geography.
Leo (*aged 11*) What good's geography?
Mother (*aged 50*) Do you know how much it costs to send you there?
Leo (*aged 11*) Take me out, then.
Mother (*aged 50*) What would your father say?
Leo (*aged 11*) (*crossly*) What do you say, Mother?
Mother (*aged 50*) You'd better go down. He's waiting. I'm going to have a lie-down—one day, you'll be grateful...

Lights down on Mother

Leo (*reflecting*) Homesickness must be the worst affliction parents can lavish on a child—years of sadness and pain—actual physical pain—while all the love in you hardens and goes solid. You build a high wall to protect yourself from the other boys—snotty kids who think you're a sissy because you wet the bed and you don't like sport. You store up a mountain of anger, bitterness and regret—(*Pause*) Later on of course you can let it out slowly and pointedly. Not that it matters because by then you've already been labelled an oddball and a black sheep and nothing you can do will change that—only confirm it. But at the time you struggle through, with a little help from *Treasure Island—Lord of the Flies—* books that will take you anywhere but back to that cold, lonely bed at night—the iron-framed dormitory bed with the crisp white hospital corners—corners done with your own tiny hands under Matron's critical gaze. (*Pause*) Something died in me in that place—I thought I'd got over it—but now it's back—only this time release will not come at the end of term—I didn't know if it would ever come—and that was the hardest thing of all to bear...

Lights fade on Leo. Spotlight back up on Mother, aged 79

Mother (*aged 79*) I'm having my hair done on Friday. What's left of it. D'you think they know something I don't? I have this desire to get them to give me a blue rinse—I always wanted a blue rinse—just imagine—laid out in virginal robes with my "Blood of Dracula" lipstick and a blue rinse. Frances would go ballistic! (*She laughs until she has a coughing fit. She splutters then recovers. Pause*) That was nursie with the bib and the baby beaker. Little sips of water and a damp sponge round your mouth every couple of hours. (*Pause*) Water! What I would give for a large gin. I must be completely detoxed by now—first time in years—wherever I end up, I hope they appreciate it. (*Pause*) No-one ever mentions Leo. (*Pause*) Someone told me a story once about an elderly relative who took a long time to die. She was very ill for months and during that time one of her sons was killed in a car crash. The family decided not to tell her. In the last moments before her death she talked contentedly about a boat drifting towards her filled with all of her long-dead friends and relations. Suddenly she screamed and shouted out "What's Edward doing in the boat?" (*Pause*) I don't know what I should have done for Leo—whatever it was, I didn't do it. (*After a pause; quietly*) I have a bad feeling about him...

Spotlight down on Mother

Lights back up on Leo who takes a letter from his pocket and appears to read it. Then he folds up the letter and puts it in an envelope, which he props up on the table. He takes the bottle of pills out of his pocket, empties a handful of pills into his hand, swallows them, swigging from the hip flask concealed down the side of the chair

The telephone rings then stops. He takes more pills, removes his glasses and either settles back into the chair, or lies down on the floor in the foetal position

Slow fade to blackout

SCENE 2

As the lights come up, Leo is sitting forward in his chair ready to talk to the audience

Leo (*reflecting*) Apparently I just lay there for days. I don't remember much about it. A lot of people walking round the bed—making notes, emptying the bag. Mostly they just let me rest. They said that was what I needed. Back home I hadn't been able to give in to it. I was still trying to play the man of the house. Still pretending—in there—in the hospital, my only duty was to get well. Then one night, they got me up...

Nurse (*off*) Wake up, Dr Warner!

Leo I was very drowsy—and boiling hot.

Nurse (*off*) Wake up. Quickly!

Leo (*drowsily*) Why is it so hot?

Nurse (*off*) Because the patient next door has set fire to his room!

Leo That was my first real introduction to the cuckoo's nest—I don't know what Frances thought of it all...

Frances enters

Frances Why didn't you tell me?

Leo Embarrassment? Shame?

Frances You're only a doctor for God's sake. That doesn't give you automatic immunity.

Leo Imagine what Father would have said?

Frances You always have to get back at him. What did he ever do to you, apart from feed you, clothe you and send you to the best schools?

Leo I can't expect you to understand.

Silence

Frances I've had it, you know. (*Pause*) Depression—I've had it too.

Leo But I could have—no, I probably couldn't—why didn't you—?

Frances Shame. Embarrassment. You and Si were so successful. How could I admit...?

Leo Simon, maybe but— (*Pause*) You too, eh?

Frances They practically had to section you before I found out!

Leo I thought I could keep it quiet.

Silence

Frances We're not so different from her, you know—Mother, I mean—Not Simon—but you and I...

Leo How is Mother?

Frances Oddly peaceful. She knows I'm there—I'm sure of it. I read to her yesterday—she likes that—squeezed my hand—it meant a lot, that did—so I stayed on and read her a couple more chapters...

Leo Still controlling the show, then?

Frances and Leo both laugh

Frances Oh, yes!

Frances exits

Leo (*reflecting*) Then the treatment started.

The Hypnotherapist enters

Hypnotherapist Leo Warner?
Leo Yes.
Hypnotherapist I gather you have something against Group Therapy.
Leo Firstly the Group and secondly the Therapy!
Hypnotherapist Good! Good!
Leo Good?
Hypnotherapist Sorry. I was not aware of having spoke out loud. Often I hear voices and it is a considerable time before I am realizing that they are all my own.
Leo (*to the audience*) After that, I can't pretend I knew what was going on...
Hypnotherapist Are you sitting comfortably?
Leo (*sarcastically*) Then you'll begin.
Hypnotherapist Your hand—give me your hand.

Leo puts out his hand

Very tense. The other...

Leo puts out his other hand

Tense also. Lift the left. Now let it fall. And again. Let it fall. (*Pause*) Now the right. Lift. Let fall. Good.
Leo (*heavily sarcastic*) Brilliant!
Hypnotherapist Lift the left again. Now imagine that tied to your wrist is a balloon filled with helium. Close your eyes. Imagine.

Leo closes his eyes

The pull of the balloon makes your arm so light that you are unable to let it fall again. Try. You see? Now the balloon is lifting your arm higher and higher. I have the scissors in my hand and I am going to cut the string, which ties the balloon to your wrist. When the string is broken your arm will fall to your lap. So, I am cutting the string—(*Louder*) now!

Leo's hand falls. His eyes remain, as they have been throughout, closed

Now what can you see, Leo?

Beat

Leo Nothing.

Beat

Hypnotherapist What colour is your nothing?
Leo Black.
Hypnotherapist Is there an end to the blackness?

Leo doesn't respond. The Hypnotherapist clicks his fingers and Leo's head drops

How old are you, Leo?
Leo (*quietly; in a child's voice*) I'm four and a half.
Hypnotherapist Is there anyone there with you?

Leo puts his finger to his mouth gesturing the Hypnotherapist to be quiet

Who is it?
Leo (*mouthing*) Daddy.
Hypnotherpist Does Daddy know you're there?

Leo shakes his head

Why not?
Leo (*whispering*) I'm hiding.
Hypnotherapist Hiding? Is it a game, Leo? Are you playing hide and seek?

Leo shakes his head

Where are you hiding?
Leo (*whispering*) Behind the settee.
Hypnotherapist Why?

Leo starts to gnaw on his fingernails

Are you afraid, Leo? Is there someone you're afraid of?

Leo nods his head

You can tell me, Leo. What are you afraid of?
Leo (*whispering*) The box—the big box in the corner (*Beat*)—with the pictures.
Hypnotherapist Oh, you mean the television. You're frightened of the television. (*Warily*) What's Daddy watching on the television?

Leo looks worried, backs away

Come on now—it's all right—

Leo looks petrified

You're safe now, Leo—it can't hurt you. Trust me—trust me, Leo—
Leo Men—men with—painted faces and feathers—and horses and guns and things...!
Hypnotherapist (*quietly*) Cowboys and Indians! (*Looking at his watch; pause*) Leo, one more thing—are you scared of Daddy?

Leo nods his head vigorously

Why?
Leo Because I'm a naughty boy.
Hypnotherapist You're a naughty boy?
Leo I'm not good—and I'm not clever—and Daddy will go away again.

Hypnotherapist Where will he go?
Leo Work.
Hypnotherapist Does his work take him away a lot?

Leo nods his head

But he has to go to work.
Leo "To pay for my education."
Hypnotherapist It's not your fault, Leo. (*Pause*) I'm bringing you back now—breathe deeply...

Pause

Relax, slowly back—I'm going to count down from ten and when I get to zero you'll open your eyes. Understand? Ten—nine—eight—seven—six...

The Hypnotherapist exits

Leo (*reflecting*) To have to admit to being frightened of the Lone Ranger and Tonto. (*Implying embarrassment*) Next time I was six. Mother was dropping me off at school. She turned to go—sweeping off down the drive in the Jag—left me standing there with my trunk, waving at no one. The therapist said I cried then—amazing the stuff we stash away—he said he'd had to give it a happy ending, change the story for me—take me home—so that I could get on with my life. (*He pauses then bobs his arm up and down, mimicking and mocking the instructions of the Hypnotherapist*) And I thought I was the loony! Understood it was all C.B.T. these days...

Rachel enters

Leo drops his arms quickly

Rachel C.B.T.?
Leo Cognitive Behavioural Therapy.
Rachel I suppose it depends on the patient—they have to try all sorts. (*Silence*) I won't be in tomorrow.

Leo looks up

    I've got a job.
Leo A job?
Rachel Don't look so surprised. I have had jobs before.
Leo A long time ago.
Rachel Just a few hours a day. To start with. At the Community Centre.
It'll get me out of the house.
Leo That's good.
Rachel You don't mind, then?
Leo Why should I?
Rachel I don't know.
Leo I think it's a good thing.
Rachel I should have gone back years ago. I just sat back and let you
carry us all along.

A bell rings to end visiting time

    Better leave before they throw me out...
Leo You took care of the family. You did what you thought was
right.
Rachel (*getting ready to go*) I did what I thought I ought to do—
what my Mother did... (*She puts her hand up to wave goodbye*)

Rachel exits

*Spotlight up Mother (aged 79). Her hair is blue and she is wearing
bright lipstick*

Mother (*aged 79*) What do you think? Well, I like it. And I feel a bit
better today, light-headed but decidedly better. (*Pause*) When was
it...? Saturday—I'm losing count of the days—they stopped
force-feeding me and took the tube out. Frances told them to. She
finally got the message. (*Pause*) So I've been lying here waiting
to catch sight of the Grim Reaper – though my eyes are very bad
now—They've dispensed with the catheter too. I've progressed—or

is it regressed—to this season's incontinence pads. Enormous they are—I don't envy these girls—(*Pause*) So that's it. All dressed up and somewhere to go. But where? (*Breathless, with difficulty*) Had enough now—there's a limit—very dark in here—no dignity—total parasite—lingering somewhere between life and death—stuck in a corridor 'til my number's called... (*Pause*) Must be a bloody long queue!

Fade spotlight on Mother

Leo (*reflecting*) I didn't make many friends there. Let's face it, it's not a place you go to meet people. Christmas Day was the worst...

A Nurse in a paper party hat enters with a cracker, a bottle of wine and a glass. He/She hands Leo the cracker

Nurse Come on now, Leo. Make an effort. Put your hat on.

Leo takes a paper hat out of the opened cracker and puts it on

Leo Where's Ellen?
Nurse In the hospital.
Leo The hospital? Why?
Nurse She cut her knees.
Leo Her knees?
Nurse She got them muddled up. Knees and wrists.

Leo makes a resigned response and the Nurse turns away to deal with an imaginary patient

Try to eat something, Melanie. The cooks spent ages making it. It's only a small piece of potato and pushing it round the plate won't make it disappear.
Leo Why you have to sit me with the anorexics, I don't know. There's a limit to the amount of roast turkey and tinned carrots a man can eat.
Nurse That's not very charitable, Leo. (*Pause*) Would you rather sit with the other depressives?
Leo No.
Nurse Why not?

Leo Because they're so fucking miserable! This is supposed to be a
    Christmas Party for Christ's sake!
Nurse You're getting better.
Leo No, I'm not.

*The Nurse offers Leo a glass of wine which he refuses, then swigs
back a large glass him/herself*

Nurse Happy Christmas!

The Nurse exits with the glass and the bottle

Leo (*reflecting*) Art therapy... (*He sits down and takes out coloured
    pens and a piece of paper and draws a demonic face*)

*The Art Therapist enters and stands looking over Leo's shoulder.
He/she then picks up the picture and holds it with his/her back to
the audience so the audience can see it*

Art Therapist (*ironically*) Why Leo, that's wonderful! It exactly
    mirrors your depression.
Leo You really think so?

*The Art Therapist walks off with the picture while Leo follows him/
her*

Art Therapist (*with more irony*) Absolutely. Clearly you have a
    profound talent for creative self-expression.
Leo I do?
Art Therapist Look here (*Pointing at the picture, suppressing
    laughter*) The disappointment, the anger, the rage—it's all here.
Leo It is?
Art Therapist How long did it take you to do, Leo?
Leo (*pleased with himself*) Well, not long, actually...
Art Therapist (*laughing with him, completely over the top*)
    Looking at this picture, Leo—I begin to feel exactly what you're
    feeling—I begin to understand what brought you here.
Leo (*joining in the joke*) You do?

Art Therapist (*way over the top*) Yes, Leo. I really do. Just let it out, Leo—let it all out. We can help you...
Leo (*laughing*) You can?
Art Therapist (*in fits of laughter*) Absolutely. Leo—I think this is—this is probably the most imaginative—the most powerful—the most dynamic—most bloody awful...!

Leo and the Art Therapist by now are falling about laughing

The Art Therapist exits, still laughing

Leo rips his picture in two and casts it aside

Leo (*reflecting*) After I was released it was a few more months before I began to feel like my old self. I had to come off the drugs gradually, that was always going to take a while—but I'd just about reached a point where I felt ready to visit Mother...

Spotlight up on Mother

Mother (*aged 79*) Leo still hasn't been in—always was a strange one. Not like Simon—he's just like his father—chip off the old block—and the other one—what's her name—always had trouble believing she was mine. Perhaps she was switched at birth—funny old thing. (*Remembering her name suddenly*) Frances! Her father adored her—quite different from the boys—he was too hard on them—but I'd never have dared say so—Simon could handle it, but Leo—if he hadn't been away at school so much I might have got to know him... (*Pause*) Too late now—don't think he wanted to be a doctor—his father wanted it badly—(*Pause*) He's made a good living at it—tired now— still—seems happy enough—they all do—tired now—tired...

Mother lies down on the bed. Spotlight down on her

Leo gets up and walks across the stage as if in a garden. Bright lights go up on stage. There is the sound of birdsong, and an echo of laughter from the scene with the Art Therapist

Leo Then one day I was taking a constitutional round the garden—The previous night I'd had my first dream since before my illness—bizarre in the way that dreams often are—but a dream nevertheless... And I heard the birds singing. It was as if I'd never heard birds singing before. It stopped me in my tracks and I listened and looked around—the sky—the roses... (*Inhaling deeply*) Everything stood out in sharp focus—the colours seemed brighter—the sounds sharper—Suddenly it felt wonderful to be alive...

A telephone rings inside the house then stops

After a few moments Rachel enters

Rachel I'm sorry—your Mother.
Leo I knew.

Rachel looks confused

I feel sad. Strange, I never expected to.
Rachel That's good.
Leo Good?
Rachel It's as it should be. (*Silence*) You've been through a really bad time...
Leo To hell and... (*Pause*) back.
Rachel I couldn't reach you... (*Pause*) When you... I was so scared.
Leo At the time... it seemed perfectly logical.

Silence

Rachel What's it...?
Leo Like? It's like waking up every day with a blanket over your head... like being in a deep pit with daylight just about visible but no matter how hard you try, you can't climb out... like being buried alive...
Rachel (*shuddering*) Why?
Leo Who knows? (*Pause*) Work? Mother? Diet? Stress? Life? The alignment of the stars? Any combination of those? The possibilities are endless... perhaps it'll make me a better doctor.

Rachel Pity I wasn't a better nurse... I felt so helpless.
Leo But you stuck by me.
Rachel I believed we were stronger than that.

Silence. Leo steps forward

Leo I—I think it's shifting, Rachel. I don't know. It's just a feeling... of course it might come back, I can't rule that out.
Rachel Don't think about that.
Leo Just at this moment... it seems almost worthwhile. Don't laugh...
Rachel I'm not going to.
Leo It had to run its course.
Rachel That's hard for me to understand right now.
Leo Harder to explain. After the darkness... it's like being reborn, I suppose. (*Pause*) I feel a real sense of wonder at the beauty in the world... like I'm seeing everything for the very first time... simple things... trees... flowers... the blue of the sky... (*He smiles and laughs to himself quietly*) Blue... (*He starts to move towards Rachel*)
Rachel (*delighted*) Go on...

Leo is now close to Rachel

Fade in music

Leo I feel—well, exhilarated... and for the first time in ages... actually *glad* to be alive.

It is as if they are about to embrace but at that moment the telephone rings inside the house. They look at each other. Then Leo stops Rachel from setting off to answer it and starts to move towards the house

Increase music level

I'll get that.

FADE TO BLACK-OUT

FURNITURE AND PROPERTY LIST

Further dressing may be added at the director's discretion

SCENE 1

On stage: Armchair. *On it*: a hidden hip flask
Another chair
Table. *On it*: telephone
Bed
Football (**Leo**) (*optional*)

Off stage: School report (**Mother**)
Letter, envelope, pill bottle *In it*: edible pills (**Leo**)

Personal: **Leo**: glasses
Hypnotherapist: watch

SCENE 2

On stage: as before
Coloured pens and a piece of paper (**Leo**)

Off stage: Bottle of wine (**Nurse**)
Wine glass (**Nurse**)
Cracker. *In it*: paper party hat (**Nurse**)

LIGHTING PLOT

Property fittings required: nil
Interior: the same throughout

Scene 1

To open: Lights up on Leo's living room

Cue 1	**Leo** sits down on the floor and hugs himself, rocking backwards and forwards *Spotlight up on* **Mother**	(Page 2)
Cue 2	**Mother**: "I wish he'd hurry up." (*Sitting back on the bed*) *The spotlight fades*	(Page 3)
Cue 3	**Leo**: "...she'd go on forever..." *Lights up on* **Mother**	(Page 4)
Cue 4	**Mother**: "...if we keep him waiting..." *Lights down on* **Mother**	(Page 5)
Cue 5	**Leo** *stares at the wall for a few seconds* *Crossfade to followspot on* **Mother**	(Page 6)
Cue 6	**Mother**: "I don't think I can stand it." *Crossfade to lights on* **Leo**	(Page 7)
Cue 7	**Leo**: "...After that it's like drowning very slowly..." *Lights up on* **Mother**	(Page 11)

| *Cue* 8 | **Mother**: "...one day, you'll be grateful..." | (Page 11) |
| | *Lights down on* **Mother** | |

| *Cue* 9 | **Leo**: "...and that was the hardest thing of all to bear..." | (Page 12) |
| | *Crossfade to spotlight on* **Mother** | |

| *Cue* 10 | **Mother**: "I have a bad feeling about him..." | (Page 13) |
| | *Crossfade to lights on* **Leo** | |

| *Cue* 11 | **Leo** lies down on the floor in the foetal position | (Page 13) |
| | *Slow fade to black-out* | |

SCENE 2

To open: Interior lighting

| *Cue* 12 | **Rachel** exits | (Page 19) |
| | *Spotlight up on* **Mother** | |

| *Cue* 13 | **Mother**: "It must be a bloody long queue! | (Page 20) |
| | *The spotlight on Mother fades* | |

| *Cue* 14 | **Leo**: "I felt ready to visit Mother..." | (Page 22) |
| | *Spotlight up on* **Mother** | |

| *Cue* 15 | **Mother**: "...tired now—tired..." (*She lies down on the bed*) | (Page 22) |
| | *The spotlight on Mother fades* | |

| *Cue* 16 | **Leo** gets up and walks across the stage | (Page 22) |
| | *Lights brighten* | |

| *Cue* 17 | **Leo**: "I'll get that." | (Page 24) |
| | *Fade to Black-out* | |

EFFECTS PLOT

<table>
<tr><td>Cue 1</td><td>Leo: "When you're feeling OK, that is——"
Telephone rings</td><td>(Page 1)</td></tr>
<tr><td>Cue 2</td><td>Rachel exits
Outside door banging</td><td>(Page 2)</td></tr>
<tr><td>Cue 3</td><td>Leo: "...a form of shock treatment perhaps ..."
Tape of child's voice as per pp 3-4</td><td>(Page 3)</td></tr>
<tr><td>Cue 4</td><td>Leo: "I—I don't feel very well..."
Car horn</td><td>(Page 5)</td></tr>
<tr><td>Cue 5</td><td>Leo: "So I stopped going in..."
Doorbell rings</td><td>(Page 8)</td></tr>
<tr><td>Cue 6</td><td>Rachel exits
Door slamming</td><td>(Page 11)</td></tr>
<tr><td>Cue 7</td><td>Leo swigs from a hip flask
Telephone rings then stops</td><td>(Page 13)</td></tr>
<tr><td>Cue 8</td><td>Rachel: "...let you carry us all along."
Bell rings</td><td>(Page 19)</td></tr>
<tr><td>Cue 9</td><td>Leo gets up and walks across the stage
Birdsong and an echo of laughter from the
   scene with the Art Therapist</td><td>(Page 22)</td></tr>
<tr><td>Cue 10</td><td>Leo is close to Rachel
Fade in music</td><td>(Page 24)</td></tr>
</table>

Cue 11   **Leo** and **Rachel** are about to embrace   (Page 24)
                  Telephone rings

Cue 12   **Leo** starts to move towards the house   (Page 24)
                  Increase music level